CHALLENGING GRAPH ART

by Erling and Dolores

Teacher Created Resources, Inc.
6421 Industry Way
Westminster, CA 92683
www.teachercreated.com

©*1997 Teacher Created Resources, Inc*
Reprinted, 2005

Made in U.S.A.
ISBN 1-55734-096-X

TABLE OF CONTENTS

(Listed in approximate order of difficulty)

MYSTERY PICTURE DIRECTIONS

This graph art activity book is a compilation of pictures which are designed to fit graph paper squares. The child colors in the squares on graph paper according to directions on a direction sheet and a mystery picture appears.

OBJECTIVES

These activities will help a child improve on:

1. Learning how to read a graph
2. transferring a visual image
3. developing fine motor coordination

4. following specific directions
5. concentrating on a task

DIRECTIONS

1. Each child is given a blank graph sheet page and a copy of a directions page (A reproducible graph sheet is at the back of this book).

2. The child should not see the answer key picture prior to doing the activity.

3. If the direction says: Color: [Y/O] A6, C11, F2, the child follows up line A and across line 6 with his fingers until they meet in square A6. Then he colors that square half yellow and half orange as indicated on the color key; he does the same to the squares C11 and F2. He should cross out each letter number as he works. It is helpful to fold back the rows as he works in order to help keep his place.

4. The squares will vary from simple to more complex, i.e.

HELPFUL TEACHING HINTS:

1. The teacher should first provide ample opportunity for the children to try out transferring different shapes on a practice graph paper. Since errors might be made on first attempts, extra graph sheets should be available.

2. Each child's paper should be hidden from others' view while working so that another child will not see the picture before he figures it out himself.

3. The finished product will be most attractive if the child:
   a. colors solidly with crayons or marking pens
   b. does not outline the squares
   c. stays within the lines
   d. blends together squares of the same color

4. Designs with the color white should be reproduced on manila paper so that the white will show.

COLOR KEY:

R=Red	YO=Yellow-orange	BG=Blue-green	T=Tan
PK=Pink	Y=Yellow	B=Blue	W=White
F=Flesh	G=Green	LB=Light Blue	GY=Gray
O=Orange	LG=Light Green	BR=Brown	BK=Black

Mystery Picture #1

Color Key

BK = Black   G = Green   W = White
R = Red   GY = Gray

Color **G** — H6 H2 H5

Color **BK** — F9 C7 D5 D2 B3 G10

Color **R** — F7 D11 A9 E1 G3 A1 F3

Color [BK / R] — E4 D1 E2

Color [BK / R] — G8 B11 G4 C1 B2

Color **G** — H11 H3 H1

Color **R** — G11 F8 B6 A6 A5 F1 B7

Color **BK** — G5 E7 C2 D8 E10 F6 G9

Color [R / BK] — C11 E3

Color **R** — F2 G7 A11 B9 B10 A8

Color **BK** — F10 D3 G6 E5 C6 D10

Color **R** — F4 G1 A2 B8 E11 A7

Color **G** — H8 H4 H9

Color [BK / GY W] — C3   [BK / G] C4

Color **BK** — D4 C10 E9 C5 D9 C9 E8

Color [R / BK] — A3 B4

Color **G** — H7 H10

Color **R** — F11 A10 A4 B1 G2

Color [R / G] — B5

Color **BK** — F5 E6 D6 C8 D7

#1 SCOTTIE DOG

11							
10							
9							
8							
7							
6							
5							
4							
3							
2							
1							
	A	B	C	D	E	F	G	H

Mystery Picture #2

Color Key

BK = Black   B = Blue   LB = Light Blue
W = White   YO = Yellow-orange

Color	Coordinates
BK	B4 B6 E11 G5
W	D6 E3 C5 F2 E4
LB	A1 A6 B1 G2 A10 H5 H10
W/B · BK/LB	D10 G3 F9
W/YO	C1 E1
LB/BK · LB/BK	G8 F11 C11 B8
BK	C10 B5 G4 F8 D11 C8 B7 G6
LB	A3 H1 G9 H4 B2 A11 G10
W	F4 F5 C3 F6 D2 D4 C6
BK/LB	B3 C9
LB	H7 A7 A8 A2 H11 A9
W/YO	D1 F1
BK · BK/YO	F10 G7 E9
W	E7 D3 F3 D7 D5
YO/W	D8 E8
LB	G1 H2 H8 G11 A4 B9 H3
BK/W · B	E10 F7
BK/W/YO	C7 D9
LB	H9 B10 A5 H6 B11
W	C2 E5 C4 E2 E6

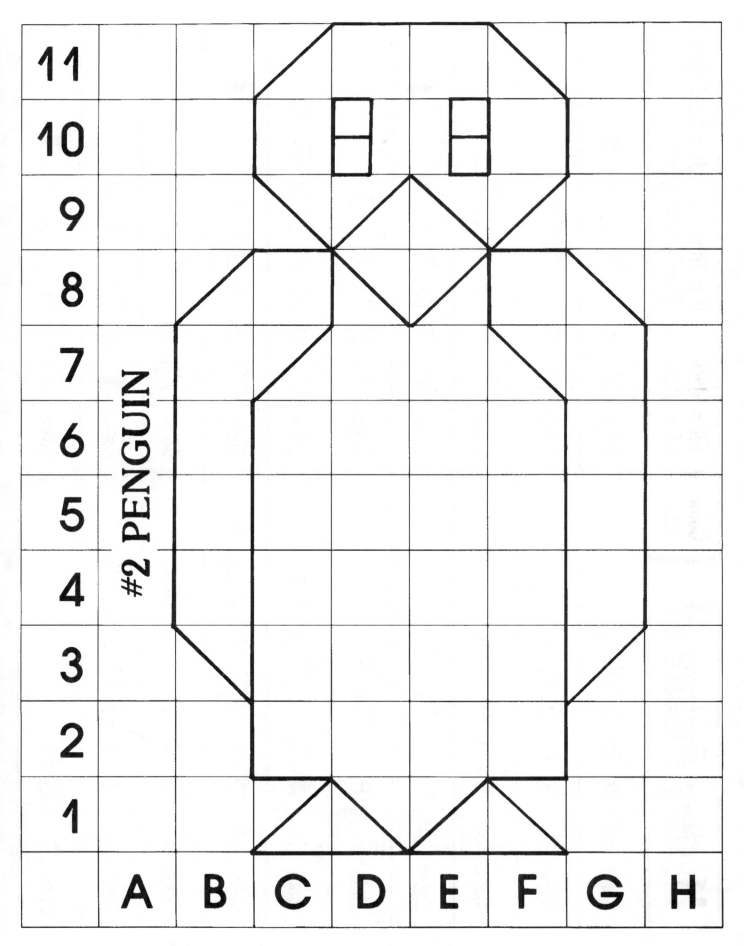

11
10
9
8
7
6
5
4
3
2
1

#2 PENGUIN

A B C D E F G H

Mystery Picture #3

Color Key

GY = Gray BG = Blue Green
LB = Light Blue W = White BK = Black

Color	Coordinates
LB	A8 D11 F10 A7 B5 B4 A1
BG / GY	G3 G7 G5 G2
GY	B10 E8 D4 D3 F2 E6 C8
BG	H2 H7 H11 H6 H3 H8
LB / GY	F9 C10 B11
LB	A11 E10 A2 B1 A9 B3
**GY / BK	W — BG / LB**	E3 G1
GY	B7 E5 C2 E1 F8 F4
BG / LB	G11 G10 G9
LB / GY	C6 B8

Color	Coordinates
GY	D1 E4 F7 D9 F6 C5
LB	E7 A5 F11 C11 D7 A3
BG / GY	G4 G8 G6
BG	H10 H5 H1 H4 H9
GY	F3 C9 E9 F5 D5
GY / LB	C1 B9
LB	A10 A6 D10 E11 B2 A4
GY / LB	B6 C7
GY	F1
GY	E2 D8 C3 D2 D6 C4

#3 WHALE

11								
10								
9								
8								
7								
6								
5								
4								
3								
2								
1								
	A	B	C	D	E	F	G	H

Mystery Picture #4

Color Key

G = Green   W = White
BK = Black   BR = Brown

Color **BK** — E2 F3 C2 G5 A5

Color **W** — C4 E6 D10 C7 C10

Color [BK/G] — B1 A10 A2

Color [BK/W] — B8 F4 E8 F10 E1

Color **G** — H1 G7 A1 H5 H10 D11 H6

Color [BK/G] — F1 G2 G10

Color **BK** — B5 B11 F11 B2

Color [G/BK] — A3 A11 E11   [W/G] B7

Color [G/W] — A6   [W/G] F7

Color **W** — B6 D1 E4 D5 D9

Color **G** — H11 G1 A9 G9 H3 H8 A8

Color [G/BK] — C11 G11 G3

Color **BK** — F5 A4 B3 F2 G4 D8

Color [BK/W] — C8 B10 F8 B4 C1

Color [W/BK] — F9 C3   [G/W] G6

Color **W** — E10 F6 D3 C6 D2 E7

Color [W/BK] — B9 E3   [W] D7

Color **G** — H2 H7 H4 G8 A7 H9

Color [BK/BR] — C9   [BK/BR] E9

Color **W** — D4 E5 C5 D6

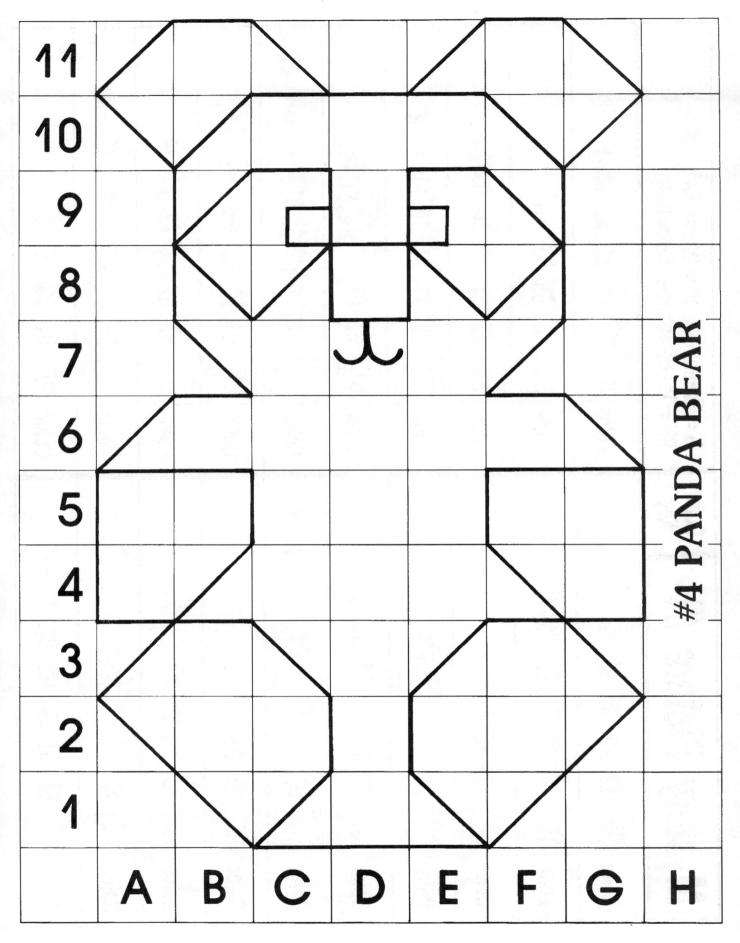

11

11
10
9
8
7
6
5
4
3
2
1

A B C D E F G H

#4 PANDA BEAR

Mystery Picture #5

Color Key

Color	Coordinates
GY	C8 H1 H5 C4
YO	F9 D3 C9 B3 C5 F4
BK [LG]	G10 G4
S [YO]	E4 [GY/YO] F11
LG	G6 E1 G1 A2 A5 G7
[YO/LG]	B2 [W/YO] E11 [YO J] E9
[GY/YO]	D2 D8 D4
YO	B8 B9 B5 B7 E3 B4
GY	H2 H7 C2 H9
LG	G5 A1 A4 G2 A10 D1 C11
LG	A11 G8 B1 A8 C1 F1
GY	C6 C10 H8 H11
[YO O]	E7 E8 [YO/GY] F2
YO	F8 F5 D7 E10 F7 D9 F6
BK [LG]	G3 G9 [YO C] E5
[LG/YO]	B10 [YO I] E6 [LG/YO] D11
GY	H10 H6 H3 H4
LG	A3 A6 B11 A7 G11 A9
YO	F3 D5 E2 C3 C7 B6 F10
[GY/YO]	D6 D10

#5 SCHOOL BUS

SCHOOL

| | A | B | C | D | E | F | G | H |

11
10
9
8
7
6
5
4
3
2
1

Mystery Picture #6

BR = Brown T = Tan LG = Light Green
PK = Pink G = Green BK = Black W = White

Color Key

Color [G] H11 H6 H1

Color [BR] C10 E5 D10 D2 D5 C5

Color [T] F6 H4 G9 D7 B3 G4

Color [T/PK] E4   [T BR / BK T] D3

Color [LG] C7 G10 D11 B8 G7 F1 A6

Color [LG/BR] B5 B10   [W/T] C4

Color [T] F8 H9 E7 B4 F5 E9

Color [LG] F11 A9 B1 C9 B6 G2 G1

Color [LG/BR] E10   [T/G] H3 H7

Color [LG/T] D9   [T/W] C3

Color [LG] A11 B11 D1 G6 F10 A3 C1

Color [G] H2 H10

Color [BR/LG] B9   [/PK T] E3

Color [BR] C2 E2

Color [LG] G11 F2 G3 E1 A8 A2

Color [T] D8 E6 G5 H8 F9

Color [BR/LG] B2   [BK T/T BR] D4

Color [LG] C11 A10 B7 C6 A4 C8

Color [T] G8 D6 E8 F7 F4 H5

Color [LG] A7 A5 A1 E11 F3

#6 SPANIEL DOG

	A	B	C	D	E	F	G	H
11								
10								
9								
8								
7								
6								
5								
4								
3								
2								
1								

Mystery Picture #7

Color Key

B = Blue   Y = Yellow   W = White
LB = Light Blue   O = Orange   BK = Black

Color	Cells
Y	A2 H1 F11 A10 A6 C1 H7 H2
O / Y (diagonal)	G8 B2
B	D7 C6 D10
LB	D3 F6 E5 C4 E8
Y / LB (diagonal)	D1 F8
Y	C5 G10 F3 H11 G5 A4 H3 H6
Y / B (diagonal)	D11 C11 B9 E10
B	C8 B7 E9 C10
B / Y (diagonal)	B6 B10 D9
Y	G11 F10 H8 G6 E1 A5 A3
B	D6 C7 B8
W / BK / LB	C2 G9
Y / B / LB	B4 D5
LB	B3 D4 F5 F7 E4 C3
LB / Y / B	F4 E3 E6
Y	F9 F1 E11 H10 G1 E2 A11 G2
Y / LB / B	D8 G7 H4 G3
LB / B / O	E7 D2
Y	A9 A7 A1 B5

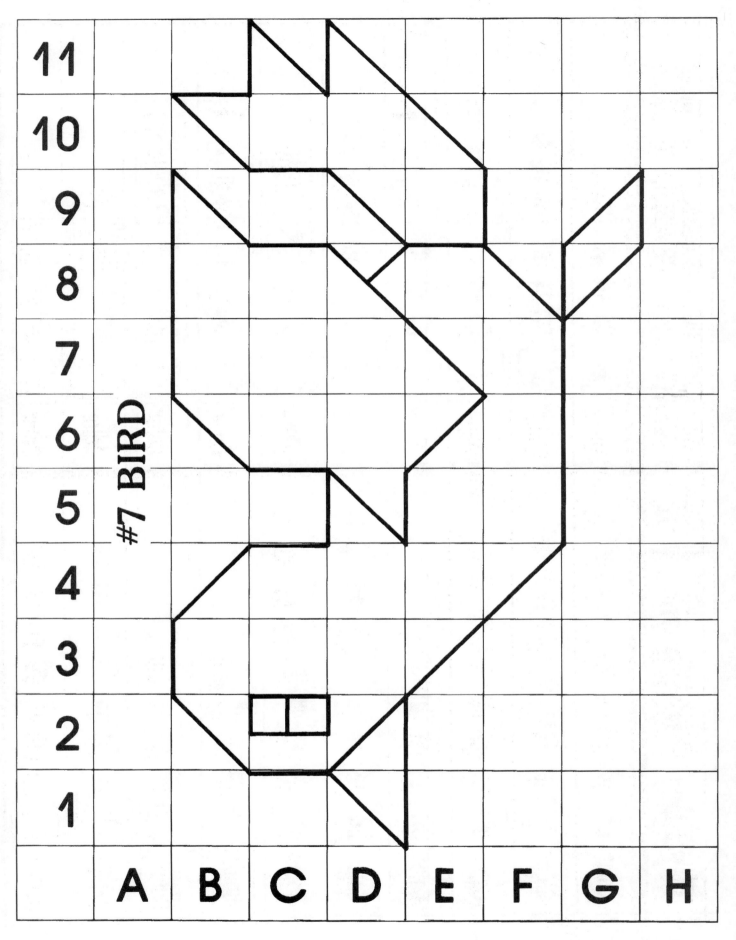

#7 BIRD

11 10 9 8 7 6 5 4 3 2 1

A B C D E F G H

Mystery Picture #8

LB = Light Blue   B = Blue   G = Green
R = Red   BR = Brown   F = Flesh

Color Key

Color	Cells
LB	A2 H2 A8 B4 D2 F11 H7 F3
R	C5 D5 E6 D7
F (LB F)	B6 F6 B9
LB	B11 F4 H6 G11 A10 B3 H11 F10
R	C7 D6 E7 E5 C6
F	D9 D10 E8 F5
BR (B/LB)	C1 E1 D11 D3
B (F curve)	D4 E4 C3 D8
LB	G9 F8 A6 G5 B10 H9 B2 G4
LB	A7 G3 H5 H10 A5 H3
B	C4 E3 C2 E2
LB / R	B7 F7
F/LB (G/BR)	C9 B1
BR/F	E9 C10
F/LB (G/BR)	C8 B5 F1
LB	G10 G6 A4 G8 H8 G2
LB	A3 B8 A11 G7 F2 A9 H4
LB/BR	C11 E11
G	A1 D1 G1 H1
BR/F (F|LB)	E10 F9

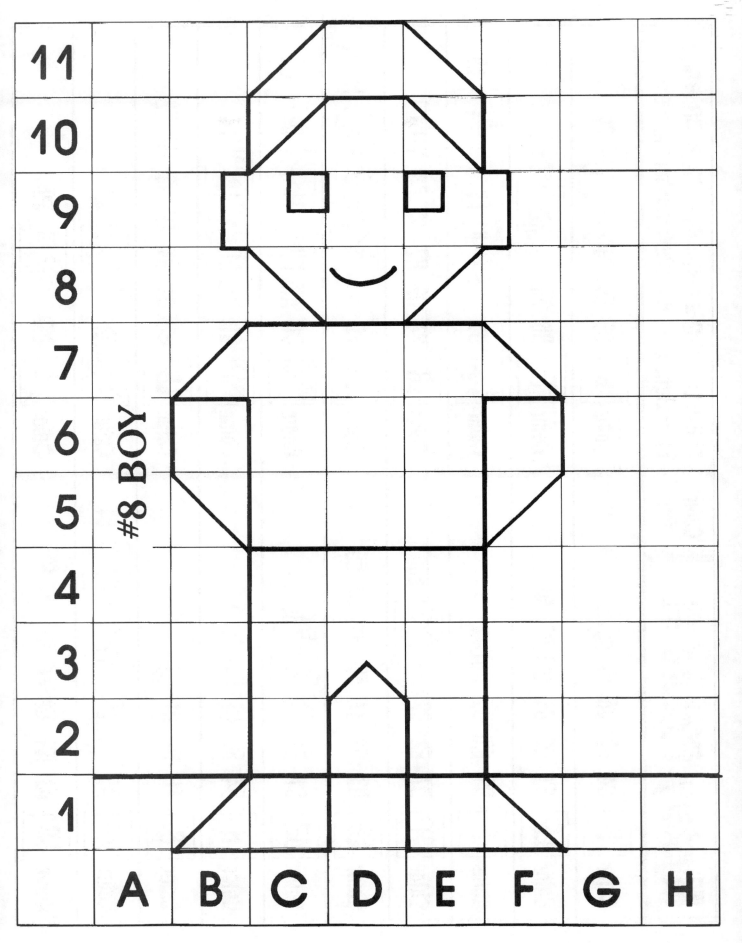

#8 BOY

Mystery Picture #9

Color [B]   C4   E7   D5   C7   D6   E5   C6   C9

Color [LB]   F3   D2   B8   G11   H5   A6   A2   B2   B6   F6   [F/LB] C8

Color [F]   C3   E3   D9   D10   [G/BR] B1   [B/F] E9

Color [R]   D7   E2   C2   [F/LB] B5   [LB] H4   G6   H7   A4   D3   B11   G8   [F|LB] F9

Color [LB]   B3   G2   A7   F8   H11   H8   G5   [G/BR] F1   [LB/R] B7   [F/LB] F5   E8

Color [BR]   C1   E1   [LB|F] B9   [LB/Y] C11   A10   F10   [F] D8

Color [B]   D4   E6   C5   E4   [LB/Y] G10   B10   E11   [LB/B] F4

Color [G]   A1   D1   H1   G1   [LB] H10   G7   G4   A11   H6   H9   H2

Color [Y]   D11   [LB/B] F7   B4   [Y/LB] A9   G9

Color [LB]   A8   H3   A3   F11   G3   A5   F2   [Y/F] C10   E10

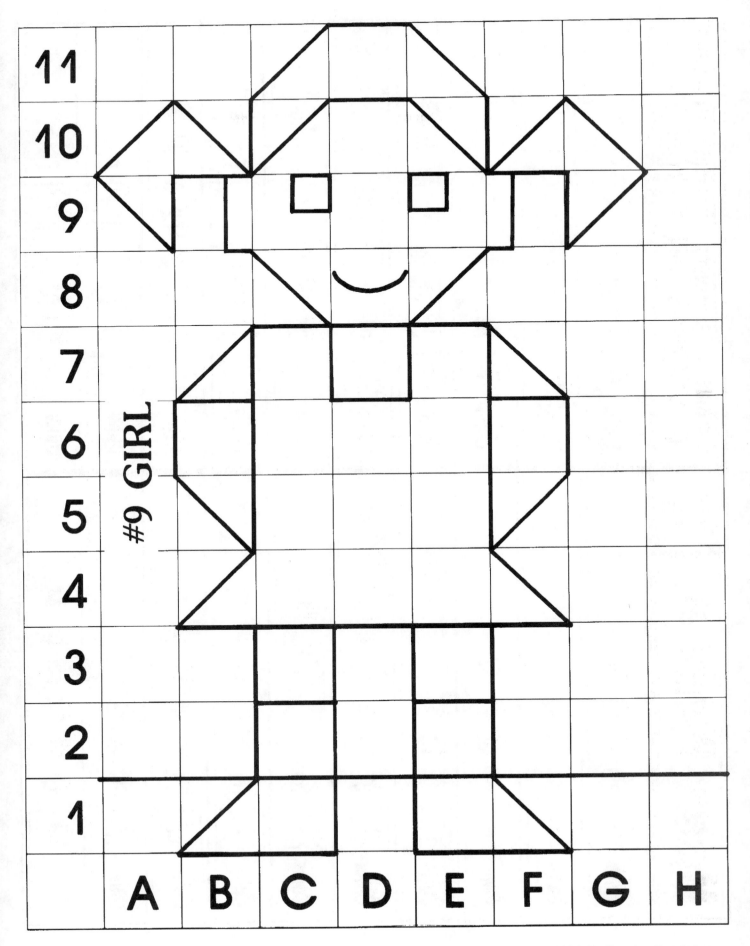

Mystery Picture #10

Color Key

Y = Yellow	T = Tan	W = White
O = Orange	B = Black	LB = Light Blue

Color [T] — H5 D8 C9 D3 H1

Color [Y] — A6 E7 F6 D6

Color [W] — F11 G10 F1 G2

Color [LB] — A9 F8 B4 F4 E2 C1 F3

Color [Y / W|BK] B7 — [O / LB] — [O / Y] C6 — [LB / O] G7

Color [O / LB] — [T / LB] G5 E8 E3

Color [T] — D9 H11 H8 D4 H7 H6 C3

Color [LB] — C10 A3 B8 D11 G8 B2 G6

Color [Y] — E5 B6 E6

Color [LB] — A11 B9 D10 F9 D1 A4

Color [W] — F2 F10

Color [W|BK / Y] B5 — [LB / Y] A7 C7 F7

Color [T] — H4 H3 H10 H9 H2

Color [LB] — B11 E10 A8 G4 D2 A1

Color [LB / T] C4 E4 E9

Color [T / Y] D5 D7

Color [W / LB] G9 G1 E11

Color [LB] — C11 B10 B3 C2 B1 A2 A10

Color [Y / LB] F5 C5 E1 — [Y / LB] A5

Color [LB / W] G11 G3 — [T / LB] C8

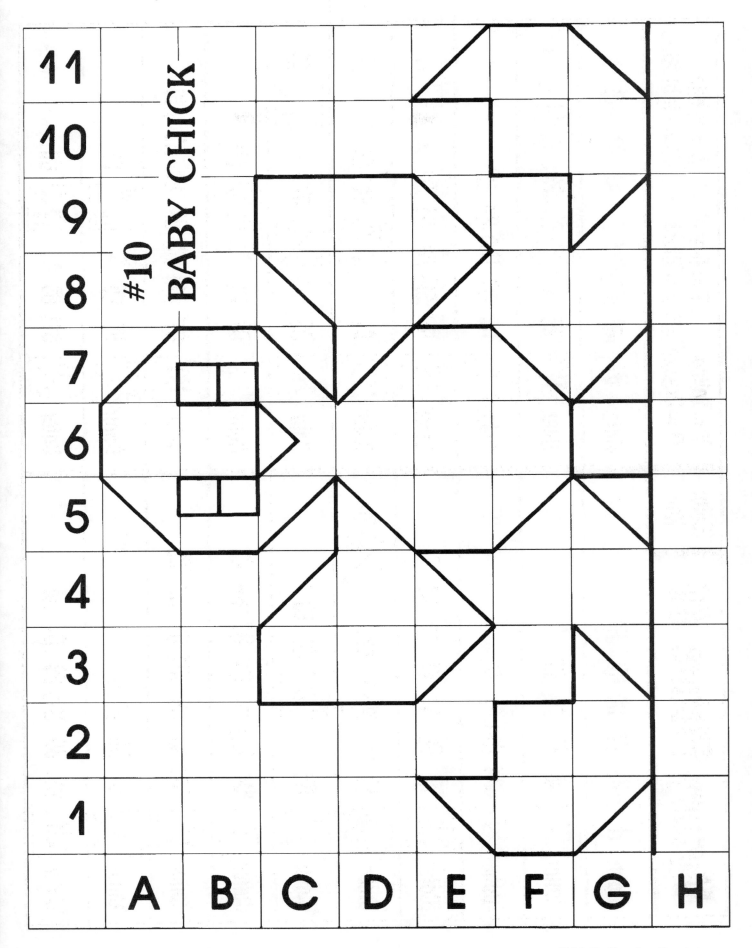

Mystery Picture #11

Color Key

G = Green	B = Blue
LG = Light Green	BR = Brown
BK = Black	
R = Red	

Color [R]: E4 G3 D6 D2 G5 F2 — A10 F11 C11 B7 A4 B2 D10 A8

Color **R** | A10 F11 C11 B7 A4 B2 D10 A8
Color **G** | C4 B3 H1 H8 H2 — F7 G6 H4 D3 F3 D5

Left side (under Color Key):

- Color **R** | E4 G3 D6 D2 G5 F2
- Color **G** | C4 B3 H1 H8 H2
- Color **[G/R] [R/G] [G/R]** | C3 H3 H6
- Color **LG** | E8 E6 C9
- Color **B** | A9 B6 A1 D1 F8 F10 C8 A11
- Color **[BK/LG over B] [B/BR]** | B9 B5
- Color **G [LG/B]** | H11 H7 D8
- Color **R** | F6 H5 E2 F4 C6 D7
- Color **[B/LG] [B] [G/B]** | E9 C10 C2
- Color **LG [G/B]** | E7 D9 G9

Right side:

- Color **B** | A10 F11 C11 B7 A4 B2 D10 A8
- Color **R** | F7 G6 H4 D3 F3 D5
- Color **[BK/LG] [R/BR]** | B10 C5
- Color **B** | F1 G8 A7 A2 B8 D11 E1 E11
- Color **[B/R] [B/R] [R/B]** | C7 G7 G2
- Color **R** | E3 F5 D4 G4
- Color **[B/G] [LG/R]** | B4 E5
- Color **G [B/G]** | H9 H10 G1
- Color **[B G]** | G11 G10
- Color **B** | A3 B1 A6 B11 E10 C1 F9 A5

#11 WORMY APPLE

	A	B	C	D	E	F	G	H
11								
10								
9								
8								
7								
6								
5								
4								
3								
2								
1								

Mystery Picture #12

Color Key

BR = Brown   G = Green   LB = Light Blue
R = Red   GY = Gray   BK = Black

Color	Cells
G	H8 A4 H1 B1 H3
R	D9 E5 E2 C8 E10
LB	F1 B10 A6 C3 D1 F11 C10
GY	C6 G10 G5 G1 C7
GY / LB (diagonal)	C9 C5
G	H2 H11 H6 A1 B3 H7
BR	F2 C2 — LB / GY (box) E11
R	D5 E6 D3 D7
GY / BK / LB	F3 F8 E4 E9
LB	B8 F5 C4 A11 A7 F7 B5

Color	Cells
R	D4 E7 D8 D6
LB	B7 A5 F10 D11 F6 C11 A10
GY	G4 G11 G7 G2
G	H5 A3 H10 H9 A2 H4
GY / BK / R — LB / BK / GY	E3 E8 F9 F4
LB / G — G / BR (box)	B4 B2
LB	B11 A9 C1 B6 A8 B9
GY	G6 G8 G9 G3
R / LB — R / BR	E1 D2
LB / R (diagonal)	D10

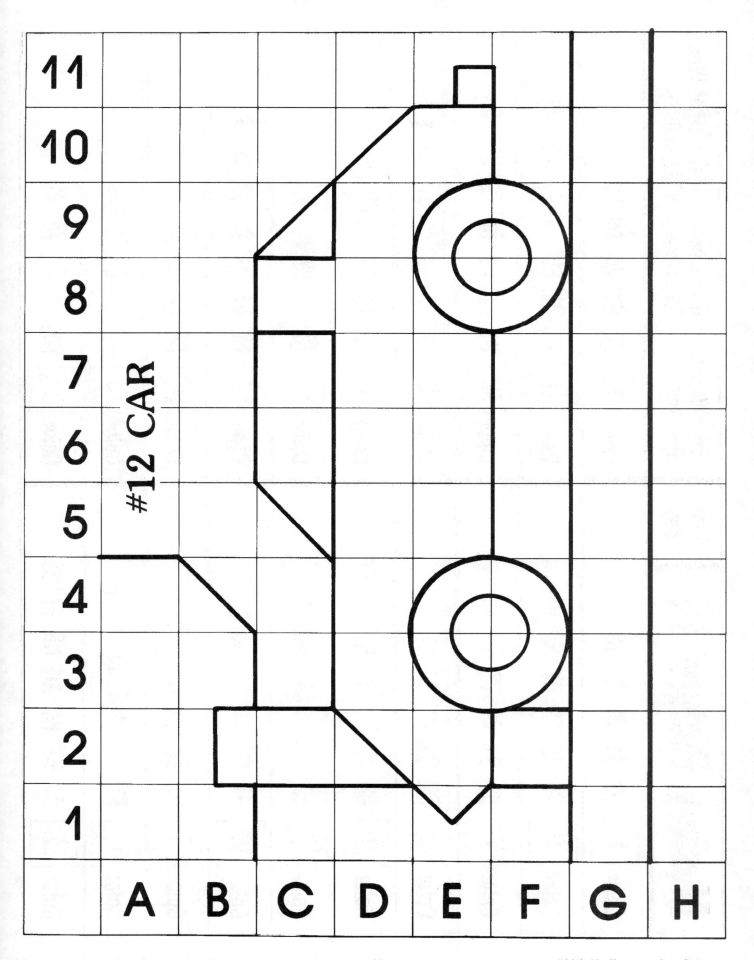

11 10 9 8 7 6 5 4 3 2 1

#12 CAR

A B C D E F G H

Mystery Picture #13

Color Key

B = Blue   R = Red   BR = Brown   Y = Yellow
W = White   BK = Black   O = Orange

Color	Cells	Color	Cells
B	H3 G9 H5 F11 B8 A4	B	H11 G10 H4 A6 B9
W	F1 G6 E4 D8 F7 G4 B6	R	F10 D10 E11
Y	D2 G8 B2 C3 C2	W	G1 F5 D6 F4 F2 B1 G3
R	E10 C10 D11	[O/W/Y] E8 [B/W] G5 G7	
B	H2 A3 B11 H7 H10 A7 C11	[W/BK] D9 E7 E6 E5	
[W/BK] E9 [B/W] B5 B7		[W/B/Y] F8 [W B] F9	
W	H1 C1 A1 D5 B4 D7	W	F6 D4 D1 E1 F3 C6 E3
[W/Y] D3 E2 [W/B] G2		[B/Y] A2 [W/Y] B3	
[BR/W/B] C8 [B W] C9		[BR W] C4 C5 C7	
B	A9 B10 H8 A10 H6	B	A8 H9 G11 A5 A11

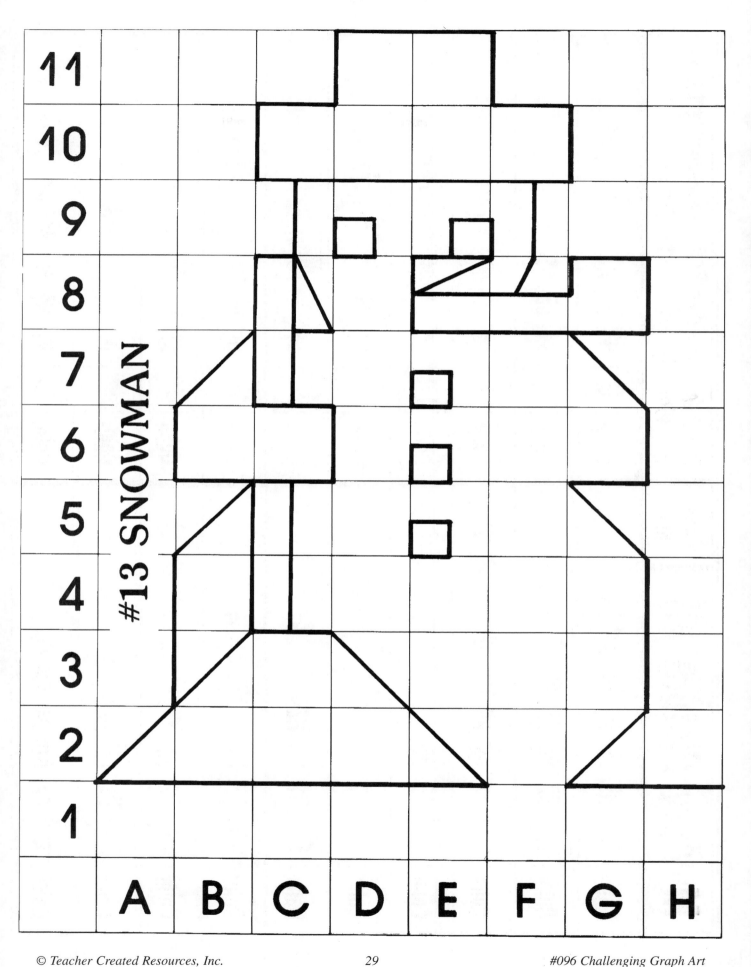

Mystery Picture #14

Color Key

Y = Yellow R = Red LB = Light Blue
O = Orange G = Green

Color	Coordinates	Color	Coordinates
G	H9 E11 H4 H10 H11 H8	G/LB	H3 H5 H7
G/LB	G2 F1 F7 G8	LB▷Y	B4 B5 B6
LB	A5 C11 A11 G7 B2 E1 C3 G4	O/LB	E8 E10
R	E3	LB	A4 B1 A1 B8 B11 D1 A9 B7
Y	C5 D5	Y	C4 C6 F2 F8
LB/G	F9 E5	LB/G	E4 E2
O	D8 E9	R/LB	D10 D9
G	H1 H6 H2	O	C10 C8 C9
Y▷R	D4	LB/G	F6 F11 G10
LB▷R	D2 D3	O▷LB	D6 G3 G5
LB	A8 D7 B9 G11 C7 G1 A6 A3	LB/Y	
G/LB	D11 F10 E6	LB/G	
LB/G	F3 F5 G9	LB	A10 A2 A7 B3 C1 B10 G6 C2

#14 TULIPS

11
10
9
8
7
6
5
4
3
2
1

A B C D E F G H

Mystery Picture #15

Color Key

F = Flesh O = Orange BK = Black W = White
B = Blue R = Red LB = Light Blue Y = Yellow

Color [F] — B7 E9 G4 H6 H7 D5 C3

Color [R] — E6 D4 D6   **Color [LB/Y]** — D2

Color [O] — G10 B9 G8 F10 D10

Color [B] — H11 A11 A3 A4 H1 H4

Color [LB] — C1 C2 F1 F2   **Color [R/F]** — C5 E7   **Color [O/F]** — C9

Color [F] — F8 D9 E3 A6 F3 C8 F6

Color [B/O] — B11 C11 D11   **Color [B/LB]** — B2

Color [O] — B10 B8 E10 G9 C10

Color [R] — E4 C4 F4

Color [B] — A1 H5 H3 A5 H2 A2

Color [B/O] — G11 F11 E11

Color [F] — F7 G5 D3 B4 C6 B5

Color [BK|W] — D8 E8   **Color [O/F]** — F9

Color [O/B] — H10 H9 H8   **Color [Y/LB]** — E2

Color [F] — G7 E5 C7 A7 G6 B6

Color [O/B] — A8 A9 A10

Color [F/R] — D7 F5   **Color [B/LB]** — B1

Color [LB/B] — G2   **Color [LB/Y]** — D1   **Color [B/LB]** — G1

Color [F/B] — G3   **Color [F/B]** — B3   **Color [LB/Y]** — E1

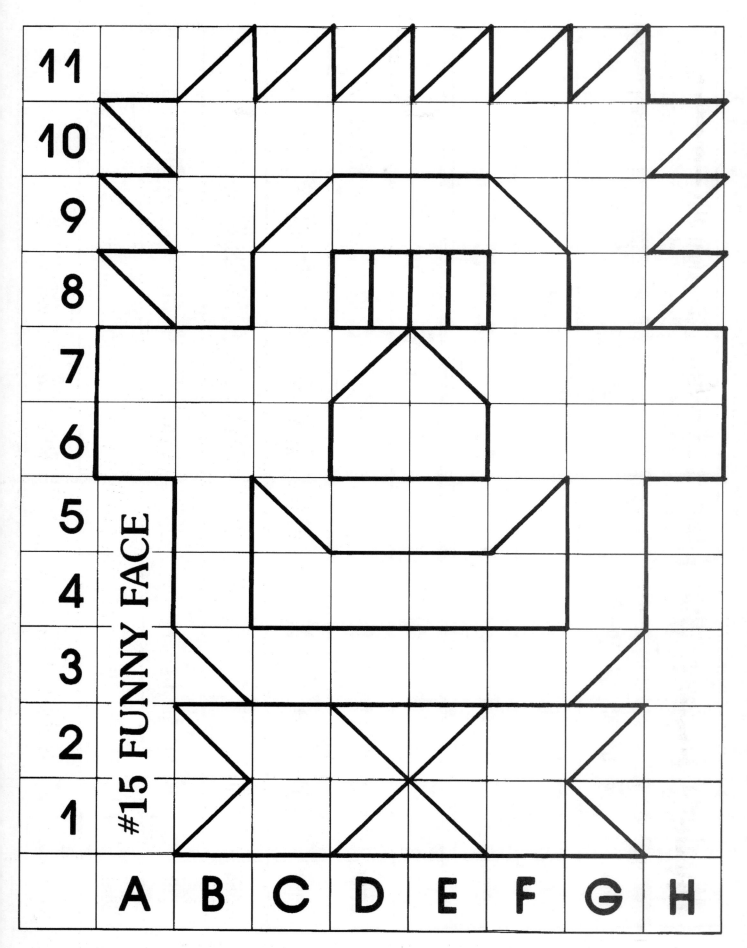

Mystery Picture #16

Color Key

BR = Brown LB = Light Blue W = White
T = Tan BK = Black G = Green

Color [T] F4 G5 B5 C2 E9 C8 F8 C4
Color [W/BK | BR/T] E8 **[BR\G/G] A2** **[T/BR] C7**

Color [BR] G8 E10 C6 B7
Color [LB\BR] A7 A8 E11

Color [LB\BR] A3 **[T/BR] F7** **[BR\LB] G10 H9**
Color [LB] C11 A10 H10 H3

Color [BK/W | T/BR] D8 (smile) D7 (smile) E7
Color [T\LB] G3 **[T\LB] B3** **[LB/T | T/LB] A4**

Color [LB] H11 A6 B11 H5 F11
Color [G\T] E2 B2 **[G\T] G2** D2

Color [T] G4 F2 E4 B4 D9 C3 D4 F3
Color [G] H1 F1 B1 D1

Color [BR\T] E5 F5 G6 F9
Color [BR] E6 F10 C10 B8 G9

Color [G] H2 E1 A1 G1 C1
Color [BR\LB] A9 B10 D11 H7 H8

Color [BR\T] D5 C5 B6 C9
Color [LB\T] A5 **[T\LB] D3** **[T\LB] E3**

Color [BR] D10 B9 F6 G7 D6
Color [LB] G11 A11 H6 H4

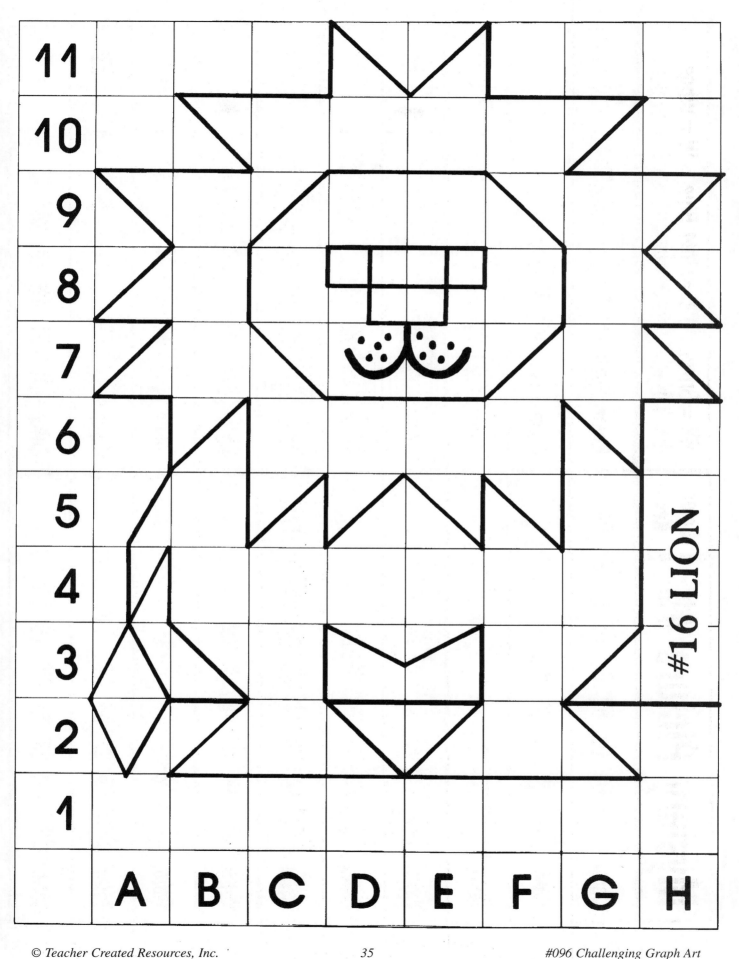

11
10
9
8
7
6
5
4
3
2
1

A B C D E F G H

#16 LION

Mystery Picture #17

Color Key

GY = Gray	G = Green
BK = Black	LG = Light Green

Mystery Picture #17

Color	Coordinates
G	G8 G11 H9 H3 G5
GY	C2 D6 E2 G3 G6 B7 E8
GY/LG (F2)	F4 F5 F2
LG	B11 A9 B1 E11 A6 A1
G/GY · GY/LG (G2)	G1 G2 D1
G/GY · LG/GY (C1)	G7 B5 C1
G	H6 H8 G9 H5 H4
GY/BK · LG/GY (C8)	D8 F9 F1 C8
LG/GY · LG/GY (F1)	C9 C10 F1
GY	D4 D7 E7 D3 E5 C4 C3

Color Key

Color	Coordinates
LG	D11 B9 A5 A11 F8 A2
G	H11 H7 G10 H10
LG/GY (C11) · G/GY (G4)	C11 G4 E1
GY/LG (B6) · LG/GY (F7) · G/GY (H1)	B6 F7 H1
LG/GY (B8 E10) · LG (F10)	B8 E10 F10
GY/LG (B2 A7) · LG/GY (D10)	B2 A7 D10
GY	B4 C7 E6 F3 E4 E9 C6
LG	F11 B10 A4 A10 A3
LG/GY (D9) · LG/GY (A8) · G/GY (H2)	D9 A8 H2
GY	D5 E3 F6 C5 D2 B3

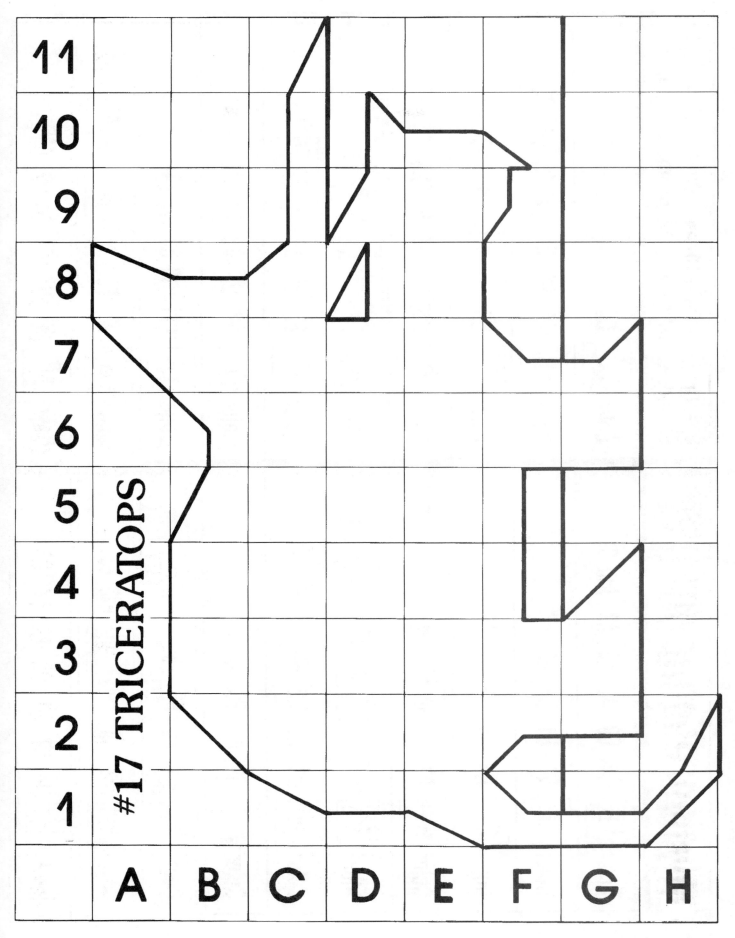

#17 TRICERATOPS

11
10
9
8
7
6
5
4
3
2
1

A B C D E F G H

Mystery Picture #18

Color Key

Color [LB] — D11 C9 A4 A3 A2 A10 C8

Color [O] — E1 E8 D3 E4

Color [GY] — G9 G6 G5 G1 G3 G10

Color [O/BR/LB] F7 — [LB/O] F11 — [O] D10

Color [LB/O] E11 — [BR/O/LB] D7

Color [G] — H11 H8 H2 H7 H5 H1

Color [W/BK/BK/W] — B9 A9 B8 A8

Color [O/LB] — F4 F5 F6 F8

Color [GY/BK/O] E2 E9 — E10 E3

Color [BR/LB] — C7 B7 A7

Color [BK/W/LB] D4 — [O/LB] D1

Color [LB] — C1 B11 B10 C4 C3 A1 C2

Color [LB/O/GY] D6 D9 D8 — [LB/O]

Color [G] — H10 H9 H4 H3 H6

Color [O/LB] F1 — [O/LB] D2

Color [O] E7 E6 E5 — [LB] D5

Color [GY] — G2 G7 G8 G11 G4

Color [LB] — C11 C10 B5 B3 A11 A6 B6

Color [GY/BK/OLB] F2 F9 — [OLB/BK/GY] F10 F3

Color [LB] — B1 B2 C6 C5 B4 A5

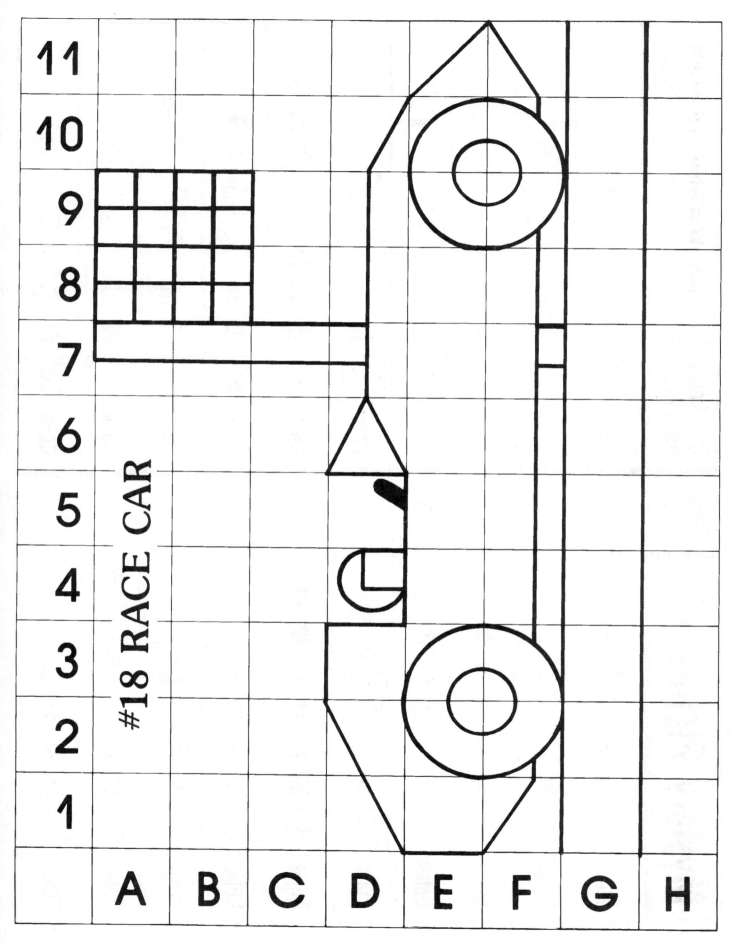

Mystery Picture #19

Color Key: O = Orange BK = Black LB = Light Blue

Color	Coordinates
[O]	G3 D4 F8 F5 D9
[O / BK]	F10 F3
[BK]	C3 B5 A10 C9 A4
[O / BK]	B2 E2 F2 G2 B3 B4
[LB / O]	G5 H4 H10
[LB]	H8 A6 A1 E1 H5 A7 C1
[O]	G4 G9 G10 D7
[BK / LB / BK]	G8 H9 C6
[BK]	C8 A3 C10 C4
[BK / O]	B11 E11 F11 B9 B10 G11
[LB]	F1 H6 H7 D1 B1 G1 H1
[BK \ LB]	C2 H2 C11 H11
[BK]	C5 B8 A9 D6
[O / LB / BK]	F7 F4 E3 E5 F6 B6
[BK \ O]	F4 E3 E5 C7
[BK / LB]	A8 A2 D2 A5 A11 D11
[BK \ LB]	D5 E4 H3 E7
[BK \ O]	D3 E6 D8 E9
[BK / O / LB]	B7 D10 E10 E8 F9
[LB / LB]	G6 G7

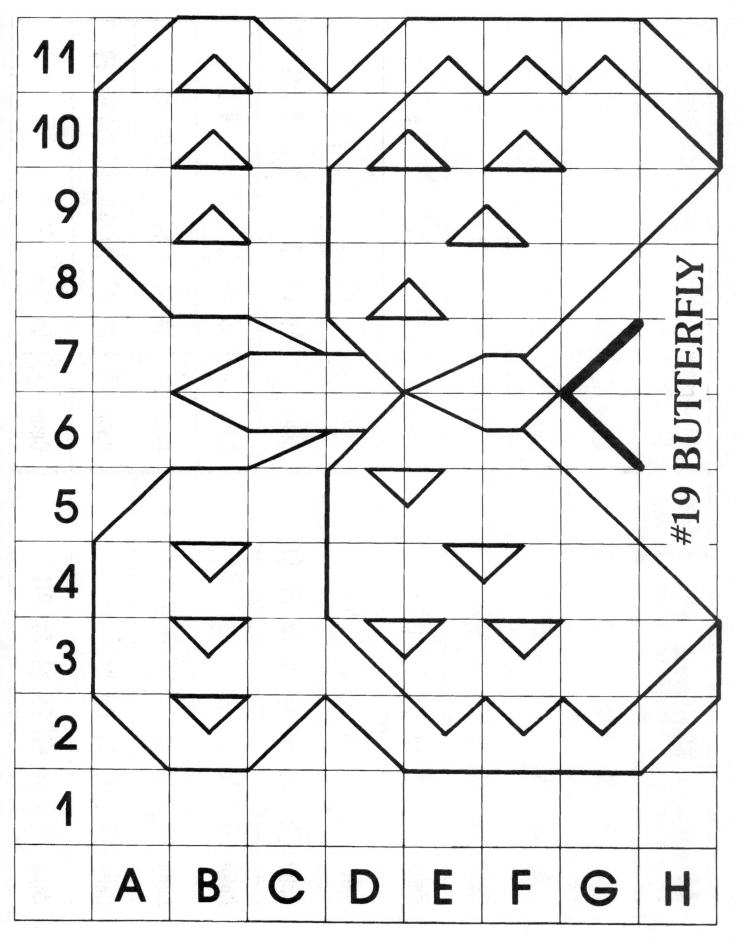

#19 BUTTERFLY

Mystery Picture #20

Color Key   BK = Black   R = Red

Color	Coordinates
[R]	G3 D9 A2 B11 F1 H4 G11 C10
[R]	D4 F5
[BK]	D7 C4 F3 E5 E2 D5
[BK]	E6 C3 D2 F4 E7 D6
[R / BK]	E4 C5 D1
[R]	H2 H9 D11 F11 G1 A5 B10
[BK R BK]	C6 F6 C9 B8
[R / BK] [R BK / R]	F9 G8 G7
[R triangle]	G5 C8 E1
[BK / R]	D3 F2
[R]	B3 F10 H8 G9 A9 A8 E11
[R]	E10 H3 A1 B9 C11 H10 A3
[R BK R]	E3 C2 F7 C7
[R BK / R]	E8 B7
[BK / R]	F8 B5 B4
[R BK / R]	G4 A6
[R / BK R]	D8 G6 B6
[R]	H5 A7 B1 G10 H1 A11 D10 H7
[R]	G2 H11 E9 B2 A4 C1 A10
[BK R / R]	H6

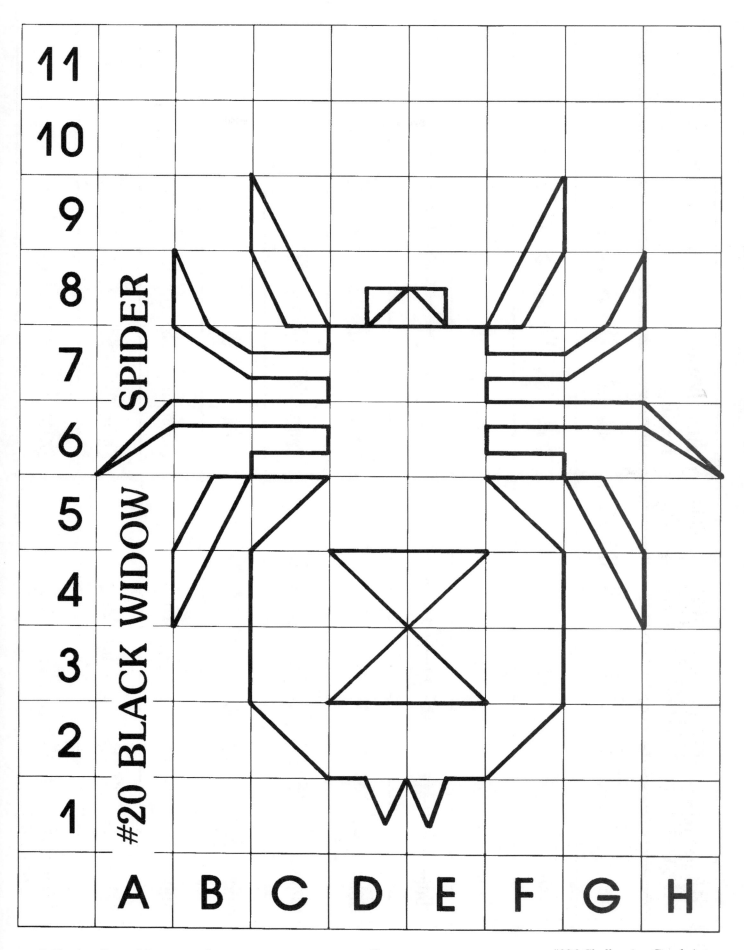

SPIDER

#20 BLACK WIDOW

Mystery Picture #21

Color [BG] G9 D11 C8 H4 D1 E11 H1

Color [GY] G7 F6 D4 G3

Color [BK/W] E4 E3 [GY/BK] G2

Color [B] A10 A2 A6 A3

Color [GY/BG] H11 H7 G10 F1 [GY/BG] C5

Color [GY/BK] F5 E1 D2 C10

Color [BG] F11 C9 H6 D9 H10 C2 H8

Color [W/BK] F4 F3 [BK/BG] G1

Color [BG/GY] G11 D8 [BG GY] C4

Color [GY] E10 F7 D5 D10 C6

Color [B] A1 A5 A11 A8

Color [B/BG] B1 B11 B5 B3 B9

Color [GY/BK] B8 [GY/BK] B7

Color [GY/R] E6 [BK/W/GY] F2

Color [GY] C7 D3 G5 E8 D6

Color [B] A9 A4 A7 [GY/BG] C3

Color [BG/GY] G6 F8 C11 [B/BG] B10 B2 B4

Color [BG] H2 C1 G8 H9 H5 F9 H3

Color [GY/BK/W] E5 [BK/B/GY/R] B6 [BK/GY/R] E2

Color [GY] D7 F10 E7 E9 G4

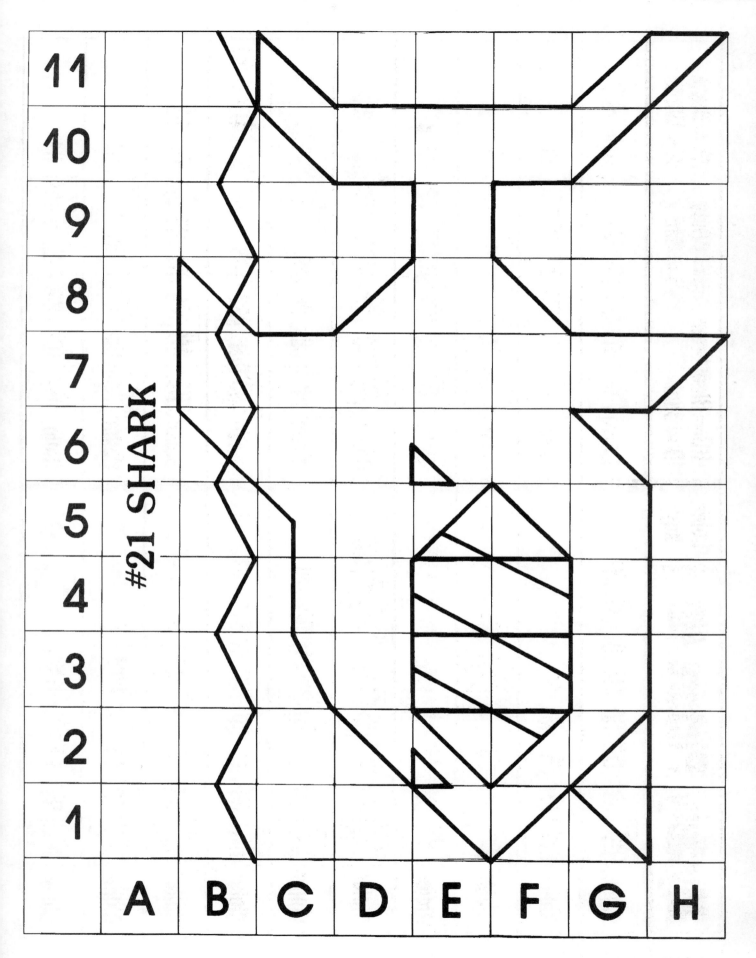

Mystery Picture #22

Coordinate	Color
G11	BG
A2	BG
C10	BG
A7	BG
D1	BG
B8	BG
A5	BG
C4	PK
E5	PK
F6	PK
E6	PK
H5	GY (diagonal) / PK
G10	GY (diagonal) / PK
C7	PK
F5	PK
B6	PK
C5	PK
F7	PK / GY / PK
B3	BG / PK / BG
C9	BG / GY / PK / GY
H8	GY / PK / GY
H1	GY
D9	BG / PK
F4	PK / BG
D7	PK / W / BK
F1	BG / PK / BG
F10	BG
B9	PK / BG
D5	BK / W
D6	W / PK
D3	BG / PK
C8	BG
A11	BG
D11	BG
E10	BG
C2	BG
B10	BG
B1	BG
H11	BG / GY
F9	BG / PK
B7	PK / BG
B4	PK / BG
E9	BG / PK
G7	GY / PK / GY
H2	PK / GY
H6	GY
B11	BG
A9	BG
F11	BG
A3	PK
A1	BG
B2	BG
A8	BG
C6	PK
B5	PK
D4	PK
G6	GY / PK
F8	BG / PK / BG
G4	PK
H7	PK
H4	GY / PK
H3	BG / PK
G9	BG / PK
G8	C3	BG / PK
E11	BG
A10	BG
C11	BG
A6	BG
C1	BG
A4	BG
H10	GY / PK
D10	PK / BG
E1	BG
E7	PK / GY
E4	PK / GY
G5	PK / BG
F3	PK / BG / PK
E8	BG
D2	BG / PK / BG
G1	PK / GY / BG
G2	GY / PK
E2	GY / PK / BG
E3	BG / PK / BG
H9	GY / PK / GY

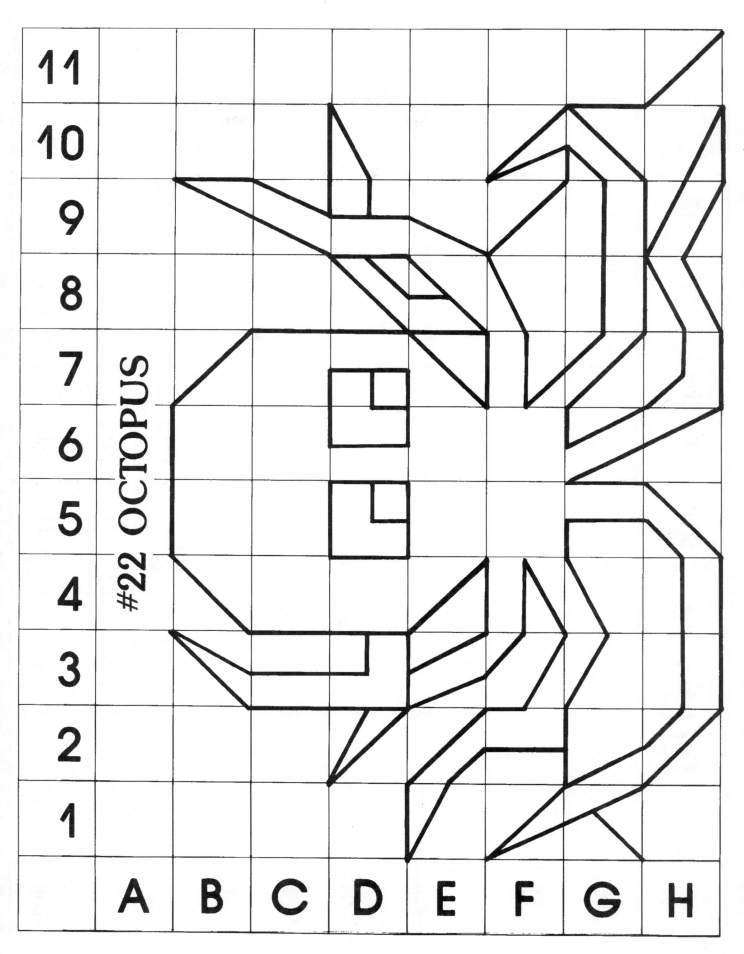

11 10 9 8 7 6 5 4 3 2 1

#22 OCTOPUS

A B C D E F G H

11							
10							
9							
8							
7							
6							
5							
4							
3							
2							
1							
	A	B	C	D	E	F	G H